How to Talk to Humans

Palmetto
PUBLISHING GROUP

WWW.PALMETTOPUBLISHINGGROUP.COM

Palmetto Publishing Group, LLC
Charleston, SC

Copyright © 2015 by Chad T. Dyar
All rights reserved. No portion of this book may be reproduced, stored in
a retrieval system, or transmitted in any form by any means—electronic,
mechanical, photocopy, recording, or other—except for brief quotations in
printed reviews, without the prior permission of the publisher.

For information on regarding special discounts for bulk
purchases, please contact Palmetto Publishing Group at
Info@PalmettoPublishingGroup.com

ISBN-13: 978-1-944313-00-5
ISBN-10: 1944313001

How to Talk to Humans

CHAD T. DYAR

Table of Contents

Introduction

COMMUNICATION IS ONE of the most important factors in building any kind of successful relationship. This book is focused on communication as one aspect of developing a successful sales career, but its lessons can be applied to every part of life. As we move through the different types of people one communicates with, I will suggest exercises to practice. You will develop necessary skills to become a better communicator. Throughout the book, I will include blogs I have published over the last several years to reiterate specific themes that go deeper into my methodology.

The art of communication has always been a passion of mine. In my first career as an opera singer, I was tasked with breaking down a complicated score to understand what it was trying to communicate. I used my voice to communicate an evolution of the character's feelings through lyrics, notes, and dynamics. I had to buy into every note and understand context in order to communicate them to the paying audience. That was only step one. I had to work with colleagues, designers, an orchestra, directors, and conductors on a mission to align our individual visions of the piece we were performing. Once we were all working together toward one common goal, we would strive to present a visibly and audibly stunning presentation to bring the crowd to its feet. As I sat at a piano with the score, the process of achieving that lofty goal began.

When I made my transition to my first business-to-business corporate sales role, I constantly looked for ways to use my previous skill set. I had developed my skills in music through years of education, practice, and performance. I learned to navigate an entirely different kind of team. I attribute a large part of my success in sales to the discipline and collaboration I learned as a professional musician. I developed a disciplined methodology as I learned how to build my own skill set and subsequently become a contributor to the creative process. Applying this methodology to careers that require a group effort can yield positive results.

Over the course of this book, I will break down the different types of people I communicate with and strategies for building relationships with them. These relationships can help you learn about yourself, your business, and the people who you are doing business with. As you read excerpts from the blogs I contribute to, you will see that I focus on big-data analytics, social selling, leadership, followership, and professional development. While this particular focus on communication may seem like a departure at times, I intend to continue writing for the rest of my career and hope to publish my thoughts on all composites that contribute to being professional.

Some of the chapters may throw you. What does communicating with friends and family have to do with how I conduct myself in a professional environment? Like art, communication is something that requires practice and evolves over the course of our lives. How we talk to ourselves and people closest to us are building blocks for how we communicate in the professional world. I am not a psychologist. I will not be quoting Freud or trying to psychoanalyze any personality types. I will not say that my way is the best way. I have had the pleasure of knowing many people who have found these methods to aid in their success. That is why I am passionate about this topic.

Preface

WE ARE LIVING in the ultimate age of communication technology. I grew up in the 80's and 90's, the era of the answering machine. You left your house to live life, whoever called could leave a message that you would retrieve when you returned home. That level of communication was an important part of my formative years.

In college, you had to go look for your friends if you wanted to meet with them. They were not always easily found, although adventure could often be found along the way. My educational and personal experiences were defined by long lectures and long conversations. Everything I attended required hours of focus. There were not distractions coming in every few seconds. In that era, even commercials on television were tolerable. Life and communication moved at the pace of real-time. Whoever was in front of you had your attention. Communication was focused on what was present. I was fortunate to have grown up in a time when I was not tied to technology that pushed or pulled me in a direction. I could explore the woods or the city for hours without having to check in with anyone. At this point, you may be asking what this has to do with talking to people; my answer is a simple one. I grew up in a time where vocal communication was necessary.

We are presently inundated with technology that keeps us plugged-in to anyone and everyone around the world. Cell phones are always in our immediate vicinity. Even though we may not speak to someone, we can maintain constant communication with him or her.

I am thankful for technology. As an adventurer, it is great to be able to have real-time communication with friends and family who are scattered to the four corners of the earth. However, having access to this kind of technology is a double-edged sword. It has drastically cut our attention span, given us the expectation of immediate gratification, and has turned our human interaction into a series of poorly spelled texts and emoticons of our moods.

Social media has given us a platform to air our grievances to the world. In my professional life, I see a constant struggle to use technology to make up for the work that an average employee is unwilling to do. Technology has become a cold connectivity that links humans together without the warmth of comforting voices and hearty handshakes. Technology reminds me of one my favorite lyrics from Rent, "(We seek) connection in an isolating age".

These are the two avenues of thought that have brought me to the place I am today. Communication has been a defining factor in my professional growth, but how do I apply those life lessons in the age of technology? That is the question I will attempt to answer in this book.

The 3 Most Important Attributes
of Being a Sales Leader

❖

I am nearing a decade of work as an Inside Sales professional. I began to explore the world of the professional salesman after my first career as a musician/performer transitioned to a lucrative hobby. I am very thankful that my early mentors preached the gospel of professional development. Continuing to educate myself has allowed me to ascend the ranks of the professional salesman to become a sales leader. After a decade of working in sales, I have come to believe that a strong sales leader, particularly an inside-sales leader, must have three major attributes to be successful.

The first attribute is creativity that leads to innovation. Innovation is a word that pops up frequently in the world of sales, but innovation is a down-the-road process that is birthed out of a creative mind. Early in my career, I found the day-to-day process of making 100+ calls with the same pitch to be mind-numbingly dull. After a year of sales, I could have been at a crossroads that ended my sales career. Instead of living in repetition, I began to experiment. I used different accents, developed a series of pitches that evolved, and created my own little sales world. They always say to treat your sales job like your own little business. Approaching my career in that way eventually led me to habitually journal my best sales experiences and embrace social selling.

The confidence I had allowed me to chase many of my ideas to fruition after moving into a leadership role. Creativity became my calling card and my new mission became instilling creativity into my sales team. Imagine a creative environment with a whole team of innovators who are always looking for a better way to achieve goals. This environment ultimately becomes a place of evolution and engagement.

The second attribute is having a head for numbers. To lead a successful sales team, it is crucial to have an analytical mind and a fully formed plan to find, analyze, and use big data. In the current era of sales, "big data" is a phrase that is starting to catch up in popularity. A strong sales leader is more than someone who was exceptional in sales or has a great personality. A strong sales leader uses the numbers to manage the team and exceed expectations. The important numbers to track are not just revenue and profit. A strong sales manager has to track and understand metrics. The numbers also include things like: the pipeline, activities, forecasting, marketing results, revenue, and profit. When a sales leader knows how to use excel and a CRM, they can be dangerous. Nobody is safe to perform near the status quo if their leader is versed in the numbers. This leads to a committed team who understands exactly where they are and where they could be. The knowledge of numbers leads to a plan to get everyone over the quota hump and on towards exceeding requirements and cashing the big commission checks. Numbers also act as a crystal ball, leading one to forecast by reviewing the pipeline, average deal size, year over year financials, and rep activity.

The third and most important attribute of a sales leader is the ability to get people to follow you. Being a sales leader means you are able to get your people to follow you into the fray. I have learned, by working for abrasive managers, that leadership is not about barking orders or intimidating people. Leadership is about getting every single *person to see and trust in your vision. It is crucial to cultivate a team mentality that embraces creativity, empowers the team with numbers, and engages each person to step up in their own way as a leader. As much faith as I have in my ideas, having a team of invested professionals who are comfortable sharing their own ideas creates a culture of innovation and trust. Leadership is about creating a culture where everyone buys into the ideas, even down to the basic metrics. We ask you to make a certain number of outbound calls for a reason. This reason is explained and encouraged with dollars and cents attached to each call. This ensures that the work is not mind-numbing call repetition but instead is an ever-evolving experiment in honing your craft.*

Sales is an honorable profession that allows creative and analytical professionals to engage both sides of their brain in order to find a better way to close the deal. Sales leaders need to acclimate themselves to sales methodology. Even though many think the old ways are best, things like innovation, big data, and social selling are here to stay. Understanding those trends and using them as a springboard to a more engaged sales team is how to exceed the sales numbers, build crucial relationships, and be a strong sales leader.

CHAPTER 1

Communicating with Yourself

How do you talk to yourself?

I HAVE OFTEN BEEN made fun of for talking to myself. I often think aloud. I read emails and blogs aloud before I send or publish them. In this case, I am asking how you talk to yourself inside your own head. Are you hard on yourself? Do you build scenarios in your mind about how situations are going to go? Whether or not you realize it, you are generally the first and third party in all of your conversations. There is what you are saying, what the person you are conversing with is saying, and then the internal dialogue playing out in your mind. Perhaps you don't have a filter and you say exactly what you think. Even then, you have an internal monologue going on at all times.

This is the point where I veer from the self-help isle to the how-to section. The way we view and relate to ourselves is the first step on the path to being a great communicator. Before we are able to motivate, inspire, or convince others of anything, we must first do these things for ourselves.

I recently read a book that addressed the "demon" in our minds that tells us things we will never do or be in our lives. I

1

believe that a mental demon is an accurate description of the first obstacle to overcome in order to be an effective communicator.

A creative mind should be a freewheeling idea machine. It is a waste of mental energy to negatively daydream about all of the changes one would make if he or she had three wishes, a superpower, or a time machine. Instead of applying all of those "what ifs" to things you can never change, what if you applied them to changes you could make NOW to your life. The "what ifs" applied as a trial and error method to improve one's circumstance can be life-changing and potentially impact the world one lives in.

As I attempt to heed my own advice, the exercise that I find most helpful is journaling. I turn off my phone, pick up my laptop, and start free form writing. Sometimes journaling becomes a list of complaints about life, other times it takes the form of a blog that is eventually published. Writing focuses my mind, it pulls out whatever has become the forefront issue, and pushes it onto the page. This is how I communicate with myself. I get to know my own hopes and dreams, I plan the adventures that I want to have, and detail the lessons I have learned through failures and success. This is the way I define the ups and downs of relationships I can have with people. When I physically articulate the intricacies of my mind, I must answer for them and confront whatever writing is produced.

Sometimes I believe we hide behind our technology. We lean on the instant gratification and form opinions about the people we work with, work for, and the prospects and clients we reach out to. We think, "Oh, I would have never been able to close that deal because the decision maker was just too challenging to communicate with." We rationalize our situation by blaming other people for failures. This attitude never leads to any kind of success. An individual is limiting access to success if he or she cannot communicate effectively. All communication starts with how you choose to communicate with yourself.

How to Talk to People

❖

Electronic communication is killing the art of the conversation and, subsequently, the art of the sale. Professionals lean into texting and emailing instead of picking up the phone. They use emojis and abbreviations, what I consider to be unprofessional. When human interaction is cut out of the sales process, it becomes order-taking 101.

On a recent inside-sales webinar, one of the sales leaders said, "When you only communicate with your prospects through email, you cease to be their sales manager and become their pen-pal." As a sales manager who fights to get reps of 50 calls a day and argues the point of speaking with someone live rather than emailing them information, that quote really stuck with me. I began to think of all of the sales books I have read, the trainings and seminars I have attended, and the thousands of calls I have listened to over the years. I realized that in the current era of instantaneous communication, maybe professionals have forgotten how to talk to other people.

The purpose of this article is to address the necessity of live communication as it relates to building professional relationships and generating business through personal connection.

The Myriad of Moods
Every morning we walk into the office in a particular mood. Whether we had a dreary Monday morning after a busy weekend or an exciting

Friday before travel, the person on the other end of the phone has had similar days.

A professional inside sales representative must interpret the mood from the beginning and immediately counter negative moods with cheer, excitement, and understanding. Putting up a mirror and smiling, even when you don't feel like it, will go a long way toward changing your mood and affecting the mood of your client/prospect. Asking a strong rapport question will help you further assess their mood and determine whether it is time to press forward into conversation, attempt to change their mood with a little wit, or reschedule the call for a better time. Always remember that there is a person on the other end of the phone who lives in a world full of complex emotions. Their bad mood isn't a personal attack on you, and their good mood isn't an instantaneous buying sign. Learning the psychology of voices over the phone and applying them to your plan of attack is a good way to develop better relationships.

Selling Yourself

Most professionals get so excited when someone answers the phone that they begin a rapid-fire data dump. They follow this by standard tie-downs, without ever having an actual conversation. Because the ratio of calls to live conversations is generally less than three to one, a live person on the line gets the blood pumping. The first thing I tell all of my new reps is that we hired them primarily because of their personalities. I have 12 very different personalities on my current team, and they need to shine through over the phone. It's ok to be a little silly or serious as long as you are being genuine. Faking a personality is as bad as the data dump.

If you can get someone live on the phone and get past the initial hello, take time to ask some questions and relate back to the answers. All of the pre-call planning in the world doesn't compare to building a genuine rapport. The person you are speaking with should feel comfortable talking to you, taking your future calls, and answering open-ended questions. These questions allow you to eventually earn their business by understanding how THEY do business and what specific needs you can fill.

The Art of the Open-Ended Question

On the subject of open-ended question, I get a little perturbed when I listen to a sales call that is filled with yes/no questions. In a recurring sales model in inside sales, we were tasked with talking to our client base at least once every 90 days and spending a year selling to a client who's business we know very little about. This can leave a lot of money/opportunity on the table. Open-ended questions are the way to find out what the client likes and does not like about how our competitors do business.

Understanding what works and what doesn't work allow us to tailor everything we offer to the client in a way that meets their needs and guarantees our future business. Start off the meat of the conversation with open-ended questions. A few yes or no questions usually shut down the client/prospect because they are being grilled instead of being conversed with. In general, people like to talk about themselves and their business. If they don't, then it may be best to find a new contact.

I Will Remember You. Will You Remember Me?

At the end of the day, how many of the people you spoke with will remember you? How many of them do you remember? If the answer is just a few, you are doing it wrong. If the answer is all of them, you are actually talking to people and not being another sales machine. People make a choice whether or not to take your calls. If they push you straight to email, it is generally a person who doesn't really want to deal with you. Another thing that will never fly with me is the attitude of, "My people only want to deal with me through email." To me, that means you have not created a meaningful relationship with your clients/prospect. They see you as an order taker instead of a partner in growing their business. Those 2-minute phone calls give us insight into the world of our clients. We can put notes into the CRM, painting a complete picture of how our clients/prospects ideally want to do business. Who buys more: the person who takes our calls and tells us about changes/needs in their business or the person who sends out an email every few months with a standard order? Make sure your clients/prospects know you, take your calls, and make a point to be remembered positively.

The Right Time to Go Online

There is a time to go online with the client/prospect. Online relation-ships should include social selling. Connect with them on LinkedIn, learn about their career path, volunteerism, and education. Research their company, find other great contacts to do business with, and like the things they post. Every time your name pops up on their newsfeed because of postings or likes, it shows you are paying attention. The more you pay attention to your clients, the more of a relationship is built to allow you to earn and keep their business.

People are not machines; ones who function mechanically are not ideal to do business with. If you walk away from calls with little to no information about the people you want to win over, it is on you for not engaging them. Engaging people at their level will create the connection that greases the wheels of business. You can read every sales book ever written and know every pitch, but you will never reach your peak performance if you do not create a real relationship with a person. Reaching your individual peak is the overall goal of inside sales in the first place.

CHAPTER 2

Communicating with Your Family and Friends

THIS IS THE chapter that throws everyone. After all, this book is supposed to be about business relationships. If you look back at the title, it is How to Talk to Humans. Your family and friends are humans (one would hope). How you communicate with loved ones forms your overall identity, considering they form your most intimate relationships. I would not typically hire someone estranged from family and friends. It says a lot about a person when they have become isolated to the point of living a solitary existence. Spending all of your free time in isolation would put you at a disadvantage. One of the strongest benefits of having close friends and family is having an additional mirror held up to you at all times.

People who are close to you are honest with you in a way most people in a professional environment would never be. Your boss might not tell you about the big piece of food stuck in your teeth, but your mom definitely would. That is a small example of a bigger idea. People who are personally connected to you can serve two huge purposes. They can first help define your strengths and weaknesses by confirming or challenging your beliefs. They also form the community where you get most of your information and shared personality traits. My sister and I look nothing alike. I am tall and broad with brown hair and blue eyes. She is petite with blonde hair and brown eyes. People do not see much family resemblance between her and I. Spend a few minutes with us, and you would know we are siblings in no time at all. We are a year apart in age and have grown up next to each other our whole lives. We communicate similarly. This influence is the same within most circles of friends and family members.

Learning to communicate effectively with those who are tied to us by blood or by circumstance is something that starts in our childhood. Our personality and communication skills develop as a result of our environment. Some families share absolutely everything with each other. This kind of over communication can become a personality trait, one I have seen in many professional settings. Inversely, there are people from families where everyone held everything inside. Those people tend to hold everything inside. They are often the ones who will walk away from their job and leave behind a group of confused bosses and teammates because they quit without ever having discussed any issues.

Being an effective communicator at home and in your personal life can go a long way towards maintaining a happy life. Strong communicators get their ideas and feelings across and are able to inspire the people around them to share in a similar way. Being a thought leader doesn't go very far unless you have some thought followers buying into your ideas. In the chapter about communicating with yourself, the exercise was to write your thoughts down in a free form way to pull the good, the bad, and the ugly out of your head. The exercise for communicating with your family and friends is both easier and more fun.

Learn the art of conversation. Turn off your phone. Are you starting to see a theme here? Make time to talk to the important people in your life. Ask them about themselves and what is important to them. It is important to learn the kinds of things that drive people. When you have a specific objective to achieve, this will become more important. My current group of friends is, what I like to call, my island of misfit toys. I have friends that are artists, great minds in business, and everything in between. I have friends that challenge my beliefs, political views, and have challenged or influenced everything in this book. That challenge has led me to learn more about my thought processes and step up to any kind of debate. In business I tend to lose respect for those who are always agreeable, I prefer the challenger personality. The challenger does not have to be obtrusive, and they often find agreement through debate and discussion. The challenger asks, "Is that the best way?" The conversation that comes out of that question pushes everyone toward improvement.

Your family and friends are your best testing ground for your ideas. They are your cheerleaders as you make redefining life choices, and they are your safety net if things don't work out as planned. Talk to them about your hopes and dreams. Make sure there are people in your life who constantly inspire and challenge you. You can find people in your professional world who act as mentors and collaborators. Your hopes and dreams tie in to your personal life and background. This means that the best support you can get is from the people who know you best, your friends and family.

7 Steps to Build Lasting Relationships

❖

In the current state of sales, tech-savvy programs seem to be incorporated in everything for analytical research. It is easy for clients to become a number in the pipeline. Even the most mediocre sales "professional" can fast talk their way into some business, but the idea is to build relationships with a loyalty that generates testimonials and referrals. Over time, this loyal client base becomes the core of the business, the first to try new products and services and the ones who will give us the honest feedback, instead of leaving us for the competition. In short, building and expanding a loyal client base anchors our business.

The purpose of this section is to take a step away from analytics and talk about good, old-fashioned relationship building. If the goal is to build a thriving business with a loyal base, it has to start with the first interaction. There has to be a development plan in place to nurture and grow the relationship over time.

1. Earn Their Trust (and Their Business) With Truth
Working from a script will never earn you someone's trust. People see through telemarketing speak and immediately become wary when someone jumps straight into making promises. In addition to being sales professionals, we are all consumers. One of the most common tactics in communicating my sales methodology is to put a sales rep in the passenger seat and role-play as the client. When a salesperson is honest and transparent, they are likely to earn your business. When they are slick and apply pressure, you walk away. Step one in building

---

relationships with clients is to earn trust. If you cannot earn trust up-front and close a deal based on dropping the price, the client will believe that to be your method of doing business. When someone beats your price or shows the client other benefits, the client will leave. You might not be the least expensive option, and that's ok. There are a lot of other differentiators in the mix. In the best possible scenario, the client likes working with you and wants you to manage their account. In time, you become irreplaceable to them by meeting their needs in a seamless and unobtrusive way.

2. Talk to Them Like Actual People

Clients are people too! Every time you call or walk into a new business, you are dealing with another human. That person may be having a great day, the worst day of their lives, or it could just be another Monday. Jumping straight into a sales pitch could be like lighting a powder keg depending on their mood and circumstances. Do not treat people like "the client".

Susie, the administrative assistant, can be your best friend or your worst enemy. Once you know that Susie is a foodie who loves her local sports team and has a kid at the state college, she could become your biggest advocate. That relationship could yield great success. One of my pet peeves is asking, "How are you doing?" straight into the pitch. There is always time for building rapport, which eventually becomes the backbone of the relationship. Also, if you want to become a champion at building real relationships, you should practice on every call and in every meeting.

3. Keep Your Promises

We have all known that flakey friend who rarely does what he or she says. Nothing will run off a prospective client faster than breaking promises. Show up if you say you are going to be somewhere. If you guarantee a custom order, make it happen. The old rule is to under-promise and over-deliver, but often I hear desperate pleas followed by sales people breaking their necks to be true to their word. There are too many factors outside of any one person's control to make certain kinds of promises. Clients trust you to do what you say you are going to do. Expectations need to be realistic and honest. This is another example of where a relationship can overcome an obstacle. If you build a trusting relationship and communicate honestly, most people will be patient and understanding as long as the issue can be resolved quickly.

4. Never Pass Clients Off

Once you have put all of the time and effort into building this relationship and become the go-to person for the client, you have to maintain continuity. Even when they call you about a service/technical issue that you are not responsible for, you have to hold their hand through the process of resolving the issue. You then follow up to make sure they are happy. The quickest way to lose trust and rapport is to pass them off by saying, "Well, I'm just your sales rep. You should really call so-and-so." They should be calling you because you are their trusted partner. It is your job to involve the right people to resolve the matter. Clients remember people who take care of them rather than paying them lip-service.

5. Don't Always Make it About Work

There is more to my life than work. I have favorite TV shows, sports teams I follow, and people that I care about. If after working with you for a period of time you know nothing about me outside of my professional role, we do not have a rock-solid relationship. I am not saying we have to be the best of friends, but I have long-standing relationships with clients who know about my life and vice versa. If I run into them in town, I know the names of their wife and children. If my company is giving away tickets for an Atlanta Braves game and I have access to a box, I call my clients who are huge Braves fans and give them that experience. From an inside sales role in an office, you cannot always get the box at the Braves game, but you can get to know your client and have a conversation that makes them remember you, like you, and want to take your calls.

6. Remember Important Occasions

This is the part of going the extra mile that makes a huge impact. Everyone should have a calendar somewhere in the office. Use it to remember people's birthdays, business anniversaries, or their yearly anniversary as a client. Most people in business do not take the time to keep up with this stuff, but LinkedIn makes it incredibly easy. LinkedIn keeps up with a lot of birthdays and business anniversaries. A CRM can give you the initial date that a client's business was earned. Every year on that date, send a card or a token from your company to say thank you for the last year of doing business with me. People want to hear things like, "I appreciate you." In time, you can look back on a lot of *years of business with a longstanding client. That becomes a testimony to your ability to earn and keep business.*

7. Find Ways to Help Them Build Their Business
If you want to build your business, help your clients build theirs. Using your resources to support your clients, their causes, and their brand will build a level of loyalty beyond giving them great service. Showing up for your client when you do not have skin in the game illustrates your commitment to that relationship.

In the end, it does not have to be all about business in today's world. If you make people feel like a number, they will likely jump ship when the next company comes along. Look at the businesses that are at the pinnacle of success today. You will see businesses that focus on people. Companies are taking better care of their employees and improving company culture. Companies are sponsoring charities and events to make their communities a better place. Companies are making sure that their clients are having the best possible experience. Building relationships is the essential key to earning and keeping business.

CHAPTER 3

Communicating with Your Leadership

ATHIS POINT, YOU know who you are. You have a strong circle of friends and family around you, and have moved on to defining who you are in your professional setting. The face you present to your boss is not the same face staring at the screen as you type out your hopes, dreams, gripes, and confessions. It is not the face you present to your family and friends when you are surrounded by love and affirmation. The face you present to your boss is your professional face. The face that says I can and I will.

Communicating with the leadership of your company is a delicate balancing act. Communication in the chapters before was expected. Communication with leadership has to be earned. There are a lot of different layers of leadership. Beneath that, there are several kinds of bosses. There is the supportive boss (yay!) who wants to hear your ideas and who will work with you until you achieve the success that he hired you for. There's the absentee boss who is never around until the minute it is time to take credit for the work that was done. There is the abusive boss who loves his job because he gets to yell at people every day. I firmly believe that abusive bosses are either taking abuse at home or were cultivated in an environment where they were abused. When it comes to communication with your boss, first you have to determine what kind of boss you have. No matter which one you work for, one thing remains the same: you will have to communicate with them. Even though you are the employee, the responsibility falls to you. It's your career on the line. You can decide which type of employee you want to be. You can be the idea person who is always looking to create and innovate to find new methods to success. You can be the steady Eddie, with a consistent and acceptable output, who meets all of the minimum standards. You can be the superstar who goes above in every possible way. You can also be the squeaky wheel who blames the boss, the process, and everyone else for creating an environment where you only barely achieve the status quo. There are many other personas, most of whom would get fired. I have had the pleasure/displeasure of working with many of these over my two decades in the workforce. You can feel any number of ways about your job, your boss, and even your company, but how you communicate those feelings will determine your success.

Sometimes a job just isn't the right fit. You get hired, jump in with both feet, and it doesn't work out. Communicating effectively with the leadership can keep you off of unemployment. When a solid employee who communicates effectively is not a good fit for one position (or is in the wrong seat on the bus, as we say) the leadership will often take an interest in keeping them with the company by finding a more suitable position. People who communicate effectively with their leaders are the ones who get on major projects, get promotions, and get raises. How do I know this? I am one of those people. Communication without doing the work is complaining. Doing the work without communication is hiding in plain sight. Hard work and communication is what puts you on the path of leadership.

Let's look at some of the challenges of communicating with leadership. A few of the challenges I have faced have been: they don't listen, they think I am arrogant, they suppress me and my ideas, or they marginalize me because my position or tenure with the company. All of these things are damaging but can be overcome. How can these be overcome? They can be overcome with communication. I will preface my next few statements with a disclaimer that I generally do not support leap-frogging your direct report. In a situation where you make the choice to go over someone's head, keep the conversation positive. You may as well involve your boss from the beginning so they cannot use the situation to run you out of the company. When your boss will not communicate with you, find someone who will. Perhaps you need some advocacy in your company. I understand that the company line would be to go to HR, but that almost always, and by that I mean always, comes across as an act of aggression. In my experience I have found like-minded employees, either on my team or in similar roles within the company, to express my ideas to. If there is commonality and buy-in, the group moves forward with the idea. Sharing and presenting your ideas, in a group setting, is a way to fight the impression of arrogance. The common theme here is communication.

I will give an example. I have always been an idea guy. When I was a salesman I wanted to find the new and best way to communicate value and build relationships with prospects. I have had a couple of bosses who were "old school" and only valued a specific approach, theirs. I blended my approach with theirs and shared my ideas with my peers. I built up my success record and added to the success of my teammates. Suddenly, my methodology became the team methodology and I was able to take it further. When the numbers became strong, the buy-in from the leadership became inevitable. When communication broke down vertically, I took a horizontal approach, which led to camaraderie and success. I was able to get my way in this case. I helped my team be more successful and build a system of accountability around my new methodology, pressing me to advance it over time.

What kind of exercise can you practice to aid in communicating with leadership? This is the scary one, but you must have the dreaded DTR talk. Yes, you must define the relationship. When you speak to your boss or the leadership team, express to them how you work best, how you communicate, and question what your expectations are. You should first ask them those specific questions about themselves. As we all know, people like to talk about themselves. When you are talking about sales people, you can apply an exponential factor into that equation. Ask your boss how they prefer to communicate. Will we have weekly meetings? If I have an idea about process improvement, how should I share that? When is it appropriate for me to come to you? Who would be the appropriate party to ask in other situations? I know those questions seem intimidating, but they are setting you up from the get-go for establishing an open dialogue with your leadership.

You can be the employee that comes in and doesn't rock the boat. The world always needs the steady Eddies in the mix. But if you want to set yourself on a path of purpose and growth, you have to execute a plan to be communicative with your leadership. This level of communication will establish your reputation and often pull you into the mix for future planning. On a side note, my career has surpassed some of the bad bosses I used to work for years ago. The ones who were lazy or didn't care to listen are working in a place where the culture some-how supports lazy and unresponsive managers. Being a strong communicator is a skill that the upper leadership looks for as people move up or move on when upper level positions need to be filled. Walk in the door with a plan to communicate. If you haven't done that already, it's never too late to start.

How to be the WORST Sales Manager in the World

❖

Coming up in sales, I had some incredible managers. My first inside sales job was an unusually #blessed experience. I had a manager who not only cared about every single member of her team's success, but who also took the time to individually coach each of the new hires. I found early success in sales because I worked for the right people. These amazing sales managers helped lay the framework for how I approach my current position.

I learned a lot from my great managers. I have learned just as much from the terrible ones. Almost every sales professional I know has had at least one terrible sales manager. I have had just a few in my life. They have left a lasting impression on me and have defined how I approach my career. I took some of the more damaging characteristics to compile a list of how to be the worst sales manager in the world, and the things I avoid at all cost.

1. Micromanage Your Team

Being a sales professional requires a good deal of freedom to build your own pipeline and develop your own relationships. Having a superior who consistently micromanages can slow your productivity. I tell each member of my team to think of their region as their own business and their quota as their own budget for running that business. Make sure the team has all of the tools to be successful. Once your team is equipped, encourage them from a distance and check in with them often on successes and challenges. You can be an active and engaged manager without micromanaging every aspect of your team's work lives.

2. Take Credit for the Work of Your Employees

I once had a manager who took credit for every major deal I closed. He went as far as putting his name next to his sales reps names on deals and in senior staff meetings. He would say, "My rep and I closed this large deal." Meanwhile, he was never on a call or in a meeting with the client. It killed my morale in that position because no matter what achievements I made, he took credit for them. The lack of appreciation led to me taking my talents elsewhere. To this day I go overboard to make sure that when someone on my team has a major achievement, their name and the details of their success is passed all the way up the ladder to the president of the company.

3. Don't Show Appreciation for Over-Achievement

Employees should be expected to show up and do their job. On the occasions when they go above and beyond and close business that took considerable time and effort, there should be appreciation and celebration. Employees who feel appreciated are more loyal and more likely to share their successes with the team. This raises the standard of work and company culture.

4. Always Come Down Hard for Under-Achievement

A manager who constantly comes down on the team and berates them for not meeting metrics will never get the best work. Employees, first and foremost, are people. People face challenges that can affect their work. A manager that knows and understands his team, and works to build an individual process for each of them to succeed, will maintain a stable team over time. I have seen too many employees let go prematurely because they didn't understand the position or weren't coached by their manager on how to be successful.

5. Talk More Than You Listen

This one is a no brainer. A blowhard manager that thinks they know all or constantly lectures their team only inspires daydreaming. The sales team is in the trenches. Day by day, they develop languages and tactics that need to be shared. I consider a great team meeting to be a meeting where I only need to comment, rather than speechify.

6. Ignore the Ideas of Your team

Sales managers are in their position for a reason. I like to think that I have a lot of great ideas. Through the years, I have learned that brainstorming and sharing my ideas with the team will turn out positively every time. When everyone brings ideas to the table, everyone feels more invested. In the last year, by letting team members contribute to our contest ideas, marketing efforts, and sales strategies, I have seen interest and the buy-in grow leaps and bounds.

7. Don't Keep Track of Your Team's Daily Numbers

It is my opinion that a good manager knows where every member of your team stands on a daily basis. There, I said it! Every metric that your team is responsible for, including their daily revenue, should be at your fingertips all day. If you see numbers slacking, you should be able to isolate all information and intervene to ensure time is not wasted. Staying on top of the numbers has a very positive impact on the leadership.

8. Lock Yourself Away From Your Team

Sales professionals need access to their manager for ideas, help, and to step in and occasionally close deals. Managers who stay behind closed doors cannot have a strong impact on daily numbers. I meet with my team daily. In addition, we have a group chat to keep a constant dialogue for encouragement and quick answers. Sales professionals are more likely to take risks when they know their manager has their back.

9. Insist That the Ways Things Have Always Been Done is the Best Way

The hardest sales environment I have ever worked in was one where the older boss wanted things done the old way. He discouraged use of social media for selling and even came down hard on me for communicating with clients via email. I am an outside-of-the-box kind of guy. His old-school mentality temporarily stifled my spirit. The way business is conducted is always evolving. To stay relevant, one must evolve as well. I eventually transitioned to working for a progressive tech company known for their methodology of pushing the envelope. I thrived in this new-age atmosphere. When looking to improve your communication skills, it is important to understand sales methodology of the past, present, and where the sales world is headed.

10. Never Stay Current and Inspired by Reading New Articles and Books on Sales Methodology

I don't understand professionals who do not look for ways to educate themselves in their field. Professional development should be a daily ritual, like morning coffee. You need to read about your market, the state of the economy, and trends in the vertical markets that you work in. In a management role, you also need to read about developing people. Managers can come off as lazy and arrogant when they ride on past success and don't continue to learn.

I worked for a man who was once part of a very successful tech company going public. In his next role, he sat back and talked about his glory days more than he ever engaged with his team. He didn't last long in that role and his reps subsequently struggled. My team makes constant use of my bookshelf. We then discuss the methodology found in the literature. I have one rep that has a voracious appetite for books on sales. His numbers have escalated as he has adopted a lot of what he's learned. I love hearing about other peers' successes and failures that have turned into life lessons. LinkedIn has proven to be a fertile ground for idea sharing.

I would love to hear some other stories about what you have learned from a terrible sales manager.

Don't Leave Your Leadership Offline

❖

For years I have heard people talk about certain 'mountain top' experiences in their lives. That 'mountain top' could refer to either a moment of true clarity or a once in a lifetime experience. I am just getting home from a National Aftermarket Summit (aptly named) that I consider a mountain top experience, encompassing both of those feelings.

I am the junior guy on the team because I have only been in my current position for about 2 years. There is an incredible team of tenured professionals all over this country in roles similar to mine. Before this week, they were disembodied voices on the other end of our monthly Aftermarket call. Then, magic happened.

Toshiba flew us all into Charlotte, NC and, for the first time, put us in the same room. Our fantastic national training team scheduled best-practice discussions (which were mostly led by us), pulled in our top vendors for face-time, and put together a national training program to roll out within the next few months. Our leadership team was heard, supported, and empowered to share our best-practices with each other. We were united as a national team with a common mission for growing our business and national brand over the next year.

My purpose in writing this is to discuss a few of the reasons why this was so important and the national impact it is will have on the company, the leadership, and the BOTTOM LINE.

Share the Pain Points and the Secrets to Success

We all have strengths and challenges. Sometimes we do not know the limitations of either side until a new perspective has been added. My team's professional worldview expanded exponentially after sharing both pain and successes. Through sharing our pain points, we were able to offer suggestions for how we may have overcome certain challenges. Sharing our successes became the basis of the best-practice sessions. In each region, there is strength, tenure, creativity, and more than our fair share of challenges. Spending three days focusing and unifying all of our perspectives re-energized the group and gave us new ideas to take back to our teams.

Put the right people in front of each other

The Summit likely would have been an amazing success, had it only been leadership to share best practices. The event was taken to new heights by bringing in a few consultants and vendors who had time to speak. We kicked off our Summit with a dynamic LinkedIn Social Selling consultant. This led to LinkedIn coming up in almost every topic discussed for the session. All of our major vendors presented to us and participated in very candid Q&A sessions, leading us all to a deeper understanding of our importance to them. We learned of the resources and tools we could source through them because of those relationships. We now have faces to put with the names and new LinkedIn connections with people that we work with daily. There is a new level of comfort when reaching out to our vendor partners and our peers.

Let the Team Know the Company is Behind Them

A company should expect to see strong and calculable success when they schedule time, travel, and talent to support a part of the organization. Two days were devoted to working with a consultant to build a national training platform designed specifically for our teams. Anyone who reads what I post knows that I have an amazing and hardworking team, but there is always more to learn. Coming back from this experience and sharing time with people who have spent decades in my field, I have more ideas than ever. Even better than that, I have a plan. That plan was laid out and fully explained. It was built with the national leadership's ideas and best-practices in mind. It will now be fully realized by our national trainers as they come into each market to deliver the training. The leadership team went through the training materials from start to finish, sharpening our game in the process and giving us a voice in how our teams will receive training moving forward. The company's investment in this training, as well as the freedom afforded to build it together, was very important. Each of us had a chance to share our best ideas with each other. Additionally, trainers were educated on ensuring that training is consistent for everyone.

One Unified Voice

Every region in the Aftermarket operates differently. We have different leadership setups, different teams, focus on different technologies, and have different styles. The one thing we all have in common is that we wear many hats as leaders in our regions. After three days in a room together, we found common ground. The training that will be delivered will be the same for each of our teams. We achieved this by going through the entire training together and sharing our ideas. It was amazing to watch so many incredibly talented and articulate people come together as a group. It renewed our energy and purpose. I would be shocked if this fiscal year was anything less than a banner year for the entire Aftermarket.

Good Times Were Had Offline

There is nothing better than a room of people who can all share your pain and then turn around and make a running joke out of it. When you are all in the same industry, dealing with a lot of the same issues, it is easy to find humor together. The offline vendor sponsored meals and drinks, which aided in our camaraderie. As serious as the business was, I cannot remember having this much fun with coworkers since back in my startup days, when we would leave the office and head straight to the bowling alley. We got things done and had a great time doing it. I already miss all of my new friends, residing in Hawaii, Detroit, Tamarac, and everywhere in between. Moving forward, I believe we will all be connected at a deeper level. We plan to use each other as resources, combining our skills and talents to grow our regions. When we take our next step, we will come back together and prepare as a national team for what is to come.

The moral of this story is that iron sharpens iron. Companies choose their leaders for a reason. Bringing them all together, letting them work through their challenges, and sharing their best-practices makes for a stronger organization overall. I left the experience energized and excited about the feedback and support I received for my ideas, with a lot of new ideas in tow. I look forward to the coming year, feeling better prepared by the training and new relationships I have made through the Aftermarket Summit.

I hope that any of my industry leading connections reading this will consider doing the same with their national leadership groups. In the hopes of refueling and refining the purpose and voice of professionals, I would like to empower others by requesting this type of Summit within their organizations.

CHAPTER 4

Communicating with Your Peers

I TOUCHED ON THIS a little in the last chapter. Have you ever heard that iron sharpens iron? Communicating with your peers, whether they work with you or are in similar roles at other companies, is the best way to sharpen your skill set. I have always sought out groups to join that put me into an equitable community of professionals. I am a member of the AA-ISP (American Association of Inside Sales Professionals). Being part of that group has allowed me to join countless webinars, with professionals in my field from all over the country and world. There is a lot of professional momentum gained by communicating with a group of like-minded people who are pushing innovation and accessing different levels of skills and practices.

Let's begin on a smaller scale. Years ago, I worked in a startup environment. The culture was exciting. Starting from the ground up meant that there was huge opportunity to be creative in the process of contributing to the sales method- ology of the company. I frequently scheduled time with my coworkers to share ideas about different applications of our product, targeted marketing campaigns, CRM development, and general innovation. Those conversations led to amazing ideas that grew our pipeline tremendously, helped us significantly increase our sales numbers, and created an open dialogue among the team. In a culture where creativity was allowed to grow, everyone tapped into something unique and different. Whether it was someone's first job or they were a veteran sales person for many years, everyone had something to add. That was the time in my career when I learned the value of peer communication. Those coworkers became friends because we opened ourselves up to that scary place where we shared our hopes, dreams, and ideas with each other. Once those ideas were out in the open, all of our individual strengths became apparent. We became a team who relied on each other and grew together.

Peer communication can be a double-edged sword. Peers can be competitive inside a company. There is always the chance that someone is going to steal your idea and claim it for his or her own. Assessment is a valuable tool to use as you communicate with your internal peer group. This becomes even more of a factor as you manage people. When you start on a team or new members come onto the team, ask them specific questions that give you an insight to their motives. Some established people like to talk about themselves, while some in a new environment want to build the perception of their worth by telling you all about their past successes, we call this the "reading of the resume". Let this lead to a conversation about their ambitions for their current role. Is the new person someone who wants to move and shake or are they just aiming for a stable income? Once you know who your peers are and what they want, you can align yourself with like-minded people and start working together on ways to innovate. I have never understood isolated workers; they make me uneasy. Being someone who is an extreme extrovert, I might make him or her nervous as well. It has always been my goal to build a baseline of communication with everyone in my organization. That is something I continue to do to this day. Whether you work with me, for me, or in a totally different part of the company, I want to get to know you and understand your motivations. I want to see what potential there is for us to work together on some level. My constant focus is a team mentality.

There is ample opportunity to share big ideas on the larger scale, whether through communicating with peers through your local chamber of commerce or any other professional organization. As I have focused on my professional growth, one of the best life lessons I have learned is that I cannot know everything. Thankfully, I can access information by engaging with a peer group. In order to be a part of a peer group comprised of experts in their fields, I will have to be a bit of an expert in a few things myself. To have access to the best, you have to be willing to give as much as you take. When you reach that place where you have access to the right people, you will be able to exhibit exponential growth by having your own strong ideas and a whole new arsenal of ideas from brains that are potentially more focused than your own.

An exercise for building and communicating with a peer group should be started in your general field and then taken to your coworkers. Accessing LinkedIn and searching for groups that share common professional interests is simple. Those are places where you can share your ideas or sample the ideas of others. If you choose to join a group where your physical presence can be known, whether through webinars or actual meetings, come prepared to share an idea or two. Feedback from people who have no skin in the game is invaluable.

Once you have some feedback and more confidence in your ideas, share them with your team. See if there is any buy-in and then work together to push for the appropriate changes. Communication requires active engagement with people. If you have something important to say, be prepared for rebuttals and constructive criticism. Remember, a single thread is weak. As you bring people into your ideas and add their support, that single thread becomes a cord of support. There will be naysayers, let them naysay until they are hoarse (see what I did there?). If you have faith in your ideas and a community of people who support and believe in them, it will trump negativity.

Are You Good at Sales?

❖

The question of whether one could excel at sales was once an easy yes or no question. That question is currently much more complex. Most people I know have sales experience because sales careers are readily available and often require little more qualification than showing up, I have heard the same story over and over, "I gave it a try and it just wasn't for me" or, "I love sales because it is rewarding to run my own business and make a great living based on the time and work I am willing to put in."

Giving a sales job "the old college try" and committing to be a professional are completely different animals. The art of selling is no longer a crapshoot. Sales is a highly skilled field that requires training, organization, and understanding at a level similar to most specialty fields. The problem lies in the limited perspectives of individuals who like to call themselves sales professionals.

The Profession of Sales

After more than two decades of selling, managing, and operating in the space of sales, I can say that I have nearly seen it all. I have seen the desk with the Rolodex and forty legal pads spread out with a rep flipping frantically through notes as they are trying to close business. Conversely, I have seen reps so dedicated to a technical process that they barely made a living but never missed a metric.

The common revolving door of sales people has always astounded me. I know how much it costs to onboard and train a new hire. If they do not work out, it is a costly mistake and often negatively impacts the fiscal bottom line and company culture. Below, I have listed a few obstacles to overcome when developing a sales professional.

Tradition

Tradition has no place in sales. It is a constantly changing and competitive field. Every client in the marketplace has myriad options of vendors. I am staunchly against the "we have always done it that way" business model. If a new strategy works, we continue to develop it. The mass telemarketing, "door to door knock and push", and "flood them with emails until they succumb" approaches are similarly fruitless. When you open the proverbial fire hydrant and push your reps to flood the market, you decrease real productivity and value in the marketplace. The new sales professional has a plan, product knowledge, a targeted market with a specific approach, a CRM to organize time and efforts, analytics to measure results, and a development and growth plan to get to the next level of their career.

Talk

Talk is cheap, and sales professionals are known for their words. In my younger days, I spent weeks learning phrases from elevator pitches to overcoming objections and all of the closing lines that I could memorize within a two-week course. I do not want to devalue any of this training and information, especially for anyone new to the field of sale; but it is 2015. If you know your market, products, and what sets your strategy apart from the competition, building relationships and having honest conversations are necessary. Not only will it earn you clients, they will stay longer than if you had used a fast talking bait-and-switch tactic to close a deal. I recently spoke to a new sales rep who was happy about closing a deal (not one of my team members). The very next day that deal went sideways. The rep was far more interested in getting the contract signed, than understanding and meeting his clients specific needs.

The "talk" part of sales needs to be about building the relationship. I task my team to clearly communicate what they do, state a purpose for reaching out, perform a needs analysis for how we can truly partner with our clients, and ask for the business. If the client is not in a position to immediately buy, the door remains open for future business. They often remember to call us back when there is a need because of the pleasant experience and rapport created by each of my team members.

Tools

Anyone who runs their business with a legal pad and a stack of business cards is playing fast and loose with their income. Today, every company that expects an ROI from its sales team needs to have tools in place to ensure success. Those tools should include a CRM system, an updated list of internal contacts and vendors, up-to-date pricing and product information that is readily available, and professional development options to make sure that a rep has access to learn advanced product training through company channels. When an average sales day includes deep knowledge and organization, even average sales reps can make a great living.

Although my team has an abundance of resources, the greatest tool my team uses is each other. Being the best at sales means being a good team player. Leveraging each other's product knowledge, sharing language that resonates with our clients, and creating a fully support-ive environment has leveled our playing field. Bringing new reps up-to-speed faster and educating tenured reps in new sales practices has certainly helped.

Tech

I know sales people who are computer illiterate, isn't that scary? As I continue to grow my team, I choose not to interview people who are unable to use basic programs. I generally look for people with at least some CRM experience. In a perfect world, all candidates would have a basic working knowledge of Salesforce.com and a LinkedIn account with a few hundred connections. My current team could not operate without their CRM. Beyond ordering things for us, CRM houses all customer information, including detailed notes of conversations, order history, and contact information. This precious information allows us to opt them in and out of marketing campaigns and approach them regarding equipment needs, vertical markets, contract types, and any other qualification we need to assign to the client. Tech also includes the automation piece in our ordering and marketing systems, email generation for tracking sold items, and internal process flow infor-mation. Whoever is speaking with a customer can look in one place to give them the information that they need. A legal pad could not come close to having the impact of a dedicated technological solution for managing clients business.

I ask again - Are you good at sales?

After around thirty informal interviews in the last few months, I have noticed the trend of applicants echoing one another, "I am good at *sales because I love talking to people" or, "I am good at sales because I am money motivated." After weeks of interviews, second interviews, background checks, and negotiations, guess whom I hired? I hired the people who said, "I am good at sales because I am going to show up every day, learn what you teach me, and DO THE WORK." Whether that person was the VP of sales for a successful company or the assistant manager at the GAP, that is the attitude I want to work with. Becoming good at sales is as simple as anything else. Learn your profession, manage your region, and have a plan for getting to the next level of your career. I am living proof that doing those things will help you advance.*

As always, I love hearing your thoughts and opinions. Ideally, I am hoping to be a part of a network of innovators on LinkedIn who share the best-practices on developing the profession of sales. Please feel free to challenge my ideas, as I love a good debate.

Building a Motivated Team

❖

Ideally, every sales manager wants to have a sales team of self-motivated overachievers.

This morning, I took an informal poll of my team on what motivates them. Most people replied that the thrill of helping their customers or winning new business motivates them. A few answered that accomplishment from exceeding quotas was motivation enough. The whole team likes that we are able to offer time off, Toshiba products, and the occasional cash prize.

As a manager, I believe that the base salary, commission, benefits package, and added incentive of the quarterly bonus should be motivation enough. Over the past year, I have learned that it takes a lot more energy and creativity to keep that enthusiasm alive in an inside sales environment.

I have given a lot of thought on how to keep my team motivated. Considering my team members are different ages and come from all walks of life, what motivates each sales professional is different. I have isolated a few methods that have had the greatest impact. Developing a culture of motivated employees keeps our workplace fun and fast-paced. The more successful the team is, the easier it is to keep them engaged through a steady stream of incentives. Product spiffs, weekly target contests, and individual recognition help keep people incentivized to give their best effort. Listed below are some of the ways that different motivations have positively impacted my team.

Cultural rewards

The easiest and most frequently used motivational tool in our office is the team reward. When everyone is working toward the same goal and can all win the same prize, they tend to push each other to success. Encouraging teamwork and rewarding team effort can drastically increase numbers for the month. In the last year, team mentality has been cemented in this office by focusing on unity and cultural rewards. We now have an office wide bonus for team achievement. We are all rewarded when the team works hard. Teamwork increases accountability, and suddenly everyone is invested in motivating each other.

Psychological rewards

I have a lot of employees who live or die by the amount of recognition they get on a daily basis. Some will spin off into space or give up if they are not getting consistent pats on the back. Praise is the easiest way to motivate anyone. Drawing the attention of the whole office to one person's achievement can make them feel accomplished and raises the stakes to keep up the good work. We use the "Go, (insert name here), Go!" method. When someone has a milestone success, the entire office gets an email highlighting the achievement, and then everyone goes and pats that person on the back. The entirety of my last blog was focused on developing the strengths of each team member and how having a confident team elevates the whole office. A big part of any team of confident people is the empowerment coming from individual recognition.

Individual Rewards

Sales people are competitive by nature. Now that team culture has been fully established, we have added contests for friendly rivalry in the office. Over the last quarter, we have implemented a raffle ticket contest. To take part in the contest, one had to get past a revenue target and meet several metrics requirements. At the end of the month, there was a drawing for a prize. With every month, the prize got bigger and the metrics and revenue requirements got tougher. Everyone continued to push harder, in-part because the more tickets you earned, the greater your chance to win. In the past, contests weren't especially exciting for the team because the same person would win every time. With the new approach, we have had a different winner each month. Everyone feels like they have a chance to win, so they all stay invested.

Grand prizes

Beyond the day-to-day motivational tools, there is the grand prize in the back of everyone's minds. President's Club is the ultimate reward. At the end of the year, the best of the best get the "all expense paid trip" and the opportunity to rub elbows with the national leadership and other best in class employees from all over the country. Motivating the team happens on all levels: the short term motivation of praise and incentives, the quarterly motivation with bonuses and rewards, and the long term motivation of the Presidents Club, an honor that can aid in promotion.

Appreciation and rewards for hard work has created an exciting culture of confident employees. We have these values to thank for the development of the successful team in the Aftermarket at Toshiba.

CHAPTER 5

Communicating with Your Employees

N OW THAT I am down the road in my career, I have people who work for me. As a boss, I have to decide which kind of boss I am going to be. One of the best things about being a boss is that I have been on the other side of that desk. I have stared into faces that smile, faces that were completely apathetic, and faces that never bothered to look up from their laptop. I decided from day one that I was going to be an "in the trenches" boss. I would not micromanage, but I would assert myself by learning my employees' roles, challenges, and client portfolios. I would be the boss who communicates.

Being a communicative boss is full of challenges. At this point, I realize that my current employees are going to read this book and look for any signs that I am talking about them. I will address this elephant on the page. Yes, I am talking about you. If you think it is you, it is. Guess what? It is most of you, but definitely not all. I hope that was helpful.

Opening the line of communication with employees can open the informational floodgates. I know nearly all about my sales team's families, health issues, allergies, phobias, and more personal information than I am comfortable with on any given day. I know these intimate details because I care and talk openly to my employees. I, on the other hand, tactfully control the flow of personal information into my professional environment. People feel like they really know me because I am such an active communicator.

I am now going to divulge my biggest secret. Are you ready?

If you communicate effectively and people view you as an open book, then they think you are always giving them all of the information. Did you follow that? Because I am open about so much, I can keep other parts of my life completely to myself, completely on my own terms. As a matter of fact, people who stumble across some parts of my past are often in shock because they felt they knew me completely. That life lesson helped me permanently pry my foot out of my mouth. I now lead with ideas and push the team creatively. There are no hang-ups about my personal life or choices. My faith and politics are not part of the office environment nor is anything that could challenge the level of respect I have worked to develop.

Communicating with employees is a delicate balance of power and empowerment. I cannot be their peer because I am responsible for their success, but I cannot be their foe because I am responsible for their growth as well. We again return to the art of the open-ended question. All of my employees would tell you that I often communicate with them. I ask mostly open-ended questions whether in person, over text, or by phone.

I mentioned in the last chapter that it is important to understand what drives people. Drive is the key aspect of managing people. Understanding someone's drive allows you to motivate him or her in a more concise way. The common misconception is that all sales people are money motivated, this is WRONG. I work with people who will work at a steady pace year round, maintaining acceptable numbers, but they will kick it into high gear if they receive a challenge, a contest, or some praise. If I toss out an incentive as simple as a pat on the back, suddenly we are in quarterly bonus territory. Understanding what drives employees is a game changer.

Communication also makes one aware of who is getting bored. There is nothing harder than managing bored employees. They come to work and do whatever it takes to get by. They don't add anything to the culture, seem to have no will to advance, and yet they take up a seat on this successful and creative team.

In this case, communication lets you know when someone is in the wrong role. Maybe they are bored because they have a personality and skill set more fitting for an administrative role. Perhaps they are tied up all day in customer issues because their passion is customer service. Communicating with your employees and learning the questions to ask will help you get them into the right role. There are people who are amazing at their job and in the wrong role, just like there are people who are in the right role but too lazy to achieve anything.

The exercise for communicating with employees is straightforward. Put together a list of things that you need to know, and then have a conversation with your employees regarding what they want out of their careers and lives. If your star salesperson is an aspiring performer, you may lose them at any time if that is where their passion and skill set is. Knowing these things will help you prepare for managing your team today and will keep you prepared to build the right bench for the future.

Team building is an integral part of communicating from the management position. It is no longer a one-on-one task. You are now responsible for building a culture of communication. Questions can be pushed from yourself to other members of your team. Assess their individual skill sets and refer them to each other until they begin to work as a unit.

My team building is what has given me the most success in my career. In my current role, I manage a large team of incredibly diverse individuals. They span ages, ethnicities, backgrounds, and personalities, yet they work together like a family. They constantly support and cheer for each other, even when competing in contests or for top ranking. They answer each other's questions, teach each other technology, and openly critique each other. GASP!

I absolutely let employees critique each other. It is part of my ongoing training and a crucial part of my sales methodology. Remember, iron sharpens iron. I don't want cheap plastic on my team. We role-play and critique each other as a team. One team member will frequently walk into my office and tell me that their teammate just had a killer call. Inversely, he or she may walk in and gently suggest that someone on the team needs additional coaching. When someone has any kind of a victory, we celebrate it. Failures are also valuable for communicating new lessons.

The people in my office feel free to express themselves and their ideas. When they don't work out, we assess and rework the idea or scrap it and try something new. When something works for one of them, the rest of them try it out. Maybe it doesn't fit his or her style or voice, but the culture of communicating in creative and innovative ways allow everyone the freedom to try. The side benefit of this is a transparent view of drives, passions, skill sets, personalities, and work ethics. I teach them the same tools I have covered thus far in this book. It is an evolving skill set that can be adapted to new situations and is a valuable tool in both personal and professional life.

The Creative Sales Team

❖

cre·a·tiv·i·ty (*krēā'tivədē*): The ability to transcend traditional ideas and to create meaningful new ones.

The field of sales is always about the next big idea to close business or engage on a deeper level with clients.

Throughout my life, I have been deemed a creative person. I have an extensive background in the performing arts and have always loved performing, writing, and inventing. When I was an educator, there was a summer with a considerable amount of free time. A friend and I decided to buy a keyless entry kit for a car and installed it on the back door of my house. When you came to my back door, I could click a button and let you into the house. We were young and thought we had reinvented the wheel. This was not a new invention, but our idea and the creativity we used allowed me to think about creativity and innovation. If you select a desired outcome and come up with a few different plans to get there, you CAN get there. I learned to use this way of thinking to set me apart from other people. It has been a crucial determining factor in my career throughout the years.

In my opinion, creativity is a difficult skill to teach, but it can be cultivated in an environment where it is valued. Because I value creativity, it has become a big part of my success in sales. Now that I manage people, I constantly look for ways to encourage "outside of the box" thinking and reward my team for conceiving and implementing creative solutions.

In weekly meetings, we discuss new ideas about language and tactics to close business, new marketing concepts, and cultural improvements for the office. Doing things the same way can make for a boring day. Our attitude towards ideas will translate into the relationships we have with our clients. Even when we find things that work, they need to evolve as we continue to grow the business.

All of the different people that I work with have a different set of ideas and come at challenges from different angles. My "by the books" people are wonderful with programs and metrics, while my "personality people" develop deep and long-lasting relationships with clients. Creativity splits the difference between the two groups as we share our ideas. The process-oriented people adapt to language that resonates with clients. The personality driven people lean on the process-oriented people to adapt to the metrics systems and technical platforms we use. The common theme that exists here is the energy that comes from engaging in creative thinking. Creative thinking leads to the sharing of ideas.

Creativity in Sales

It is fair to say that most sales people use price as their primary closing tool. When all else fails, drop your pants and earn the business! Low margin selling doesn't pay the bills when you earn a living that is profit based. This year, we have a few new ideas for growing our business. One of the biggest new ideas is teaching clients about their own buying cycles. Being transparent about their habits will build trust and allows us to honestly and fairly sell to them at appropriate times throughout the year. In a recurring sales model, it is not only important to keep the customers happy, but to also make the repeated buying process *conveniently streamlined. This method elevates the rep to the level of expert. Our clients have begun to express an appreciation for the new level of care they have been receiving.*

To begin the process of cultivating creativity, I started with a few questions for my team. I asked my team questions such as, "What's an experience you had personally that made you want to come back and do business again with a company?" and, "Name something that would make you pay a premium price for a product or service that you could probably get at a lower cost somewhere else." We bullet point these ideas into a discussion that generally leads to a concept and occasionally to a strategy. The fundamental ideas of strategies are pretty standard, but the practices are new and exciting. Once the campaigns are tracked for success, we see what has worked and what has not. At the end of the day, my team all feels more invested in our sales process. Over time, the team has begun to share incredible new ideas. I put a high value on people who devote time to creativity and innovation.

Creativity in Marketing

Anyone can put together a fabulous looking coupon these days with Photoshop and Internet access. Buy-one-get-one-free, percentage off discounts, and free shipping will likely get the attention of clients. We use tools like these to generate business in slower months and to introduce new products. I am not an advocate for constantly reinventing the wheel, but I enjoy adding a layer of nuance to an idea that can put your personal and professional stamp on it.

Mass emailing and couponing have their place, similarly to telemarketing with a script, but I prefer marketing tools that allow my team to engage on a deeper level with their clients. Even if we use an old methodology, I will not green light it until there is an undeniable personality stamp from the person who has designed it.

A team can make the best of a situation, even if things seem dire. My team recently lost the Internet and access to all of programs for a full day. We couldn't look up pricing, had no CRM access to get into notes and contact information for our clients, and our email went down. Our lights and phones were thankfully still up. I joked that my little bit of Native American heritage may give me an edge in sending smoke signals to other offices and warehouses that we were unable to reach via phone. That day, the team put their heads together and came up with ways to be effective. One rep opened Outlook and wrote fifty emails as drafts and sent them the next day when the Internet was back up. She received a high response rate because of the time and attention she was able to give each email. One rep pulled an old paper quote file out and closed some business with people she hasn't spoken with in over a year. One rep played Solitaire most of the day; you can't win them all. At at the end of the day, every member had a list of what to do if this ever happened again. We found a way to close business in a situation where we could have closed our doors and called it a day.

Here at Toshiba, we value creativity. We look for new ways to hit our metrics and to engage with our clients. Some of our ideas have fallen flat, but most of the time we start with a seed that grows into something new and interesting. It keeps things fun and it keeps people engaged. Finding new and faster ways to accomplish goals has allowed me to take out a few time consuming steps in our CRM process. It has helped to network my group into a larger community within our international organization. Our ideas put us in the spotlight, which keep us accountable in keeping the ideas coming and to constantly measure their successes. We have grown a potentially stagnant business model into a company of thriving overachievers, working together to come up with the next big idea. I love the challenge and adventure of working with a team of creative innovators and highly recommend making some time for a little creativity in your life each day.

CHAPTER 6

Communicating with Your Vendors

LOVE MY VENDORS, and not because they occasionally buy me a nice dinner. At the end of the day, the relationship you have with your vendors will most directly impact business with them. These are the people whose products you sell and whose services you share. These are the people you work, negotiate, laugh, and sometimes fight with to get the best possible deal. Optimally, there is an ironclad deal. Worst case, you share them with all of your major competitors and fight for face time.

In this chapter, I would like to give credit to vendors. In my career, I have known vendors who have been exceptional communicators and have been excellent at their jobs. I am thinking of one in particular who probably knows more about me than some of my employees. I currently have a vendor partner who lives on the opposite coast, yet I see him several times a year and communicate with him often. He maintains a wealth of knowledge about his products and genuinely loves what he does. He makes communication easy. He is there anytime I need anything. He responds to voicemails and emails quickly and lets me know about any major happenings in our industry.

I am going to shift focus for the rest of this chapter to the other human vendors I interact with (I will address Martians and machines in the sequel). Any form of business requires communicating. Vendors often communicate passively because of the nature of our relationship with them. We exist in two different companies with different objectives that happen to intersect in one place, but we have our own initiatives. In order to both succeed, we need a lot from each other. I personally reach out to a lot of my vendors to generate marketing campaigns, request contests, and to test pricing flexibility. It requires a unique kind of communication in order to get from hello to hell-yeah.

Communicating with yourself can be brutal. Communicating with friends and family can be emotional. Communication with the people you work with is mandatory. Communicating with vendors moves into the persuasive category of communication. In a vendor relationship, persuasion becomes more of a focal point. When speaking with clients, this skill becomes increasingly more important. The art of persuasion is using your newfound and highly developed communication skills to get what you want. Sometimes it is as easy as asking and then there is the trade-off, the quid-pro-quo method. Effective persuasion means you have the ability to get what you need by using the logic of your language.

Logical linguistics sounds like a college course you may have slept through. The power of persuasion sounds like an equally boring seminar. The gist of this concept is that you have to convert someone to a disciple of your thought process. Sound too cult-y? It's not. It's the way sales people have built a loyal clientele for generations.

This is not an easy premise. First, you have to know your stuff. People can easily poke holes in the talk bubbles that come out of your keister. When you are speaking to a vendor, you are speaking to a professional with his or her own initiatives and busy schedule. Why should they do this thing for you? This is where I insert my reasoning behind my request, the initial cost of said request, and the ideal pay-off. I get my resounding hell-yeah and then I am off to the next thing.

Before this conversation, I had put in hours of time communicating with my vendor. I made sure I understood as much as I could about our relationship, their business, and what parameters I was supposed to work within. After I am able to understand the parameters, a specific set of processes begins. I introduce my concept to a coworker, ensuring that my idea is coherent and specific enough to get traction. I then take the time to write out the bullet point objectives of the conversation. Once I get into the meeting, I am prepared. I understand what objections could come up and have a rebuttal for each. I am not asking for anything that could get either of us into trouble and have buy-in from my team. What I am asking for is specific; I lay out an objective and a time frame. I ask for a commitment at the end of the meeting. When I get the commitment, I get something even more important, respect. I generally get the win because I respected the vendor, their time, and the situation by diligently following the stated steps. This discourse leads to a better relationship with my vendor and more respect from my company.

Communication requires detail work and is generally the determining factor of success in any business dealing. Working off of the top of your head generally leads to a lethargic effort toward achieving goals. The more specific the questions you ask, the more likely the outcome. If I know I have to do step A to get to step B and so on, I will tackle each task to get to the goal. If the goal is a generic idea, the goal will be more difficult to attain.

The exercise for developing better communication with vendors is to practice discipline. Outline an objective and use methodology preparation for the conversation. Remember to assess the parameters and get buy-in from your peers. Make sure that this effort is not your very first communication with your vendor partner. Starting the relationship with a list of demands does not set the tone well for any type of relationship. Imagine if you approached a first date by saying, "Thank you for coming to dinner with me. Here are my expectations and here is my desired outcome." This is the point where you wipe the wine off of your face and head home with your delusion.

A first encounter with anyone should be met with preparation. Know what you might ask them and be prepared with some answers of your own. Spontaneity is great. I am a huge believer in adventures and have them often, but a time and thought investment is required when you are building any kind of new relationship.

How to Succeed in a Sales Environment

❖

Each time a person is plugged into a new role on the team, I immediately go through my list of how to be successful in that position. As part of a dynamic sales environment, there are always new lessons to be learned. One of our goals at Toshiba is to empower the sales team to be successful in every way. We put together a CRM and chop the information into bite-sized lists to call. We make sure employees' health and family obligations can be easily met by being flexible with time off. Training is provided and escalations have a clearly defined process flow. The sales team really only has to do one thing: SELL.

The purpose of this section is to highlight advice with an explanation of how it can benefit the team, our company, and our client base.

Time Management

Time management is an important life skill. Time management is THE key to being successful in a professional environment. Planning ahead and sticking to that plan is the best way to achieve success, especially when meeting metrics is a requirement. My team has a recommended schedule that includes times for call blocks, administrative work, and putting out fires. Building time into the daily schedule to handle unexpected issues is the best way to avoid being thrown off your game. If there are no issues, that time defaults back to more time on the phone. Time management is a discipline. We all know going to the gym for exercise will improve our health. We similarly know that making more calls will improve our numbers, but results only come from doing. Organization also makes the difference between being a busy rep and being an accomplished rep. A rep can spin their wheels until it's time to go in an eight-hour workday, or they can make a plan and effectively accomplish daily goals.

Exceed the Minimum Requirements

Sales professionals should have metric requirements to meet, including a minimum expectation of calls, talk time with prospects and clients, CRM activity, quotes, and closed business. Surpassing the minimum metric requirement is the quickest path to overachievement. Professionals who consistently fail to meet the minimum requirement are a bad fit for the position and will eventually drag down the performance of the team.

Treat Prospects Like People By Showing Interest in Them and Their Business

As we role-play to develop our conversation skills, my pet peeve has become the rapid-fire data dump. That method entails forcing your entire message across before letting someone off a call. I am not a fan of this type of selling. It has that scripted telemarketing feel. Since I work with over a dozen reps, each with diverse and interesting personalities, I encourage them to let their personality shine through on calls. The first step to getting prospects to open up is being open with them about who you are. The second step is to ask open-ended questions. That's Sales 101, right? I have led many training sessions through the years; all sessions have focused on open-ended questions to get to know the needs of clients. When I coach reps or listen in on calls, I find them consistently defaulting to telling rather than selling. Great reps use open-ended questions to get comfortable with a little bit of silence on the other end of the line.

I started my sales career as a data dumper. I knew I had precious few seconds to get my point across before the call ended. I would meekly start giving company information, and would jump to price if I felt any kind of push back. I became the dreaded "drop your pants" sales rep who sold on price over value. It didn't take long to learn that this was not the way to make a great living in sales. I eventually learned how to ask the right questions, obtain the right information, and lead the prospects down the path of closing business. Some of my former clients maintain a loyalty with me to this day because of that rapport.

Understand and Leverage Vendor Relationships
I am always learning new things from developing stronger relationships with our vendors. The vendors we work with are great regarding marketing collateral, handling pricing quotes for us, and most are willing to actually speak with our clients on a conference call to help close more business. When our clients understand the power and depth of our vendor relationships, it builds more confidence in the goods and services we are able to provide. Leveraging vendor relationships can alleviate some of our workload.

Add to Company Culture
Over the last decade, company culture has become a huge factor in success, hiring appeal, and employee and client retention. I have worked at both extremes of company culture. One office environment was cold and sterile with no planned employee interaction. Another

was a start-up with game tables and a beer fridge. We even had office-wide bowling days during business hours. Toshiba is somewhere in the middle. Every birthday and holiday is celebrated, but professionalism reigns supreme. During business hours, we work. The company culture isn't only what the company offers its employees, but what the employees bring to the business. This can range from bringing in cupcakes for the whole office to walking into the office every day with a smile. Adding to the company culture raises the overall energy and excitement of the office, putting everyone in a better position to achieve success.

Keep a Good Attitude

While this final goal may appear simple, it is probably the most important. It can put a damper on the day when I work with people who are sour or complain. Every minute dealing with negativity is a minute that could have been spent building the business. Negativity spreads and breeds office gossip, entitlement, and hurts company culture. Clients can gauge a negative attitude over the phone, which hurts the business and earning potential of the rep. In my one-on-one meetings with my team, I tell each of them to leave their problems at the door. A person's issues will still be there at 5pm. Learning to separate personal issues from business will allow you to be more successful and happier. I am certainly in a better mood when I receive a bigger paycheck. A sense of accomplishment builds confidence and yields better results.

I have recently had the great pleasure of attending webinars where inside sales leaders share practices and ask thought provoking questions. I am always open to discussion and hope to hear from sales leaders on some of the methods used to inspire their teams.

Romancing Revenue Relationships

Relationships often have similar challenges. They have ups and downs; the beginning is full of excitement and the end can be devastating. This is the year of sharing best-practices and developing an external best-in-class client service process.

Best-in-class service has a different meaning in the world of inside sales as a recurring model because our relationships run deep. Some Aftermarket account managers have over ten years of experience in the business and clients who have been with them the entire way. I am not a relationship therapist, I can only write from the perspective of someone who has had long-term business relationships and worked with a team of successful professionals. The purpose of this section is to give advice to sales professionals who are tasked to build, develop, and maintain long-term client relationships.

Be Honest and Upfront With Who You Are

Whether you have a new client or are new in your role, the first move sets the tone of the relationship. Coming into a new situation, you have no idea about the client's relationship history. Sometimes they are coming off being burned by their last vendor. Sometimes they are truly/madly/deeply in love with another vendor and happen to end up in your pipeline. Most of the time, they need more information before they make a decision about you. Some new reps are hesitant about letting a client know they are new. I think you can use that to add charm to the relationship. Let them know you have something to prove to them, to your management, and to yourself about your new role. Being new cannot and should not ever be used as an excuse for mediocre service. People understand that you cannot know what you do not know, but the new team member remains the conduit for information connecting the client with resources. Use your wit to let them know this is going to be a learning experience for both of you and actively participate by conferencing in your manager or team lead. It demonstrates honesty to the new client, builds trust early on, and demonstrates that you are still the right point of contact to get things done.

Listen to Them (Even When You Want to Talk Over Them and Explain)

Most sales people love to talk. A client asks one question and we have the entire training manual worth of information to regurgitate to the prospect/client. When a client feels like you are not listening, they shut down. Listening is different than thinking about what to say next. You should actively listen. When they are finished talking, whether it is praising your excellent work or ripping you, repeat the key phrases that stood out to you and work with them on a plan of action to keep things great, improve things, or salvage the sinking (relation)ship.

I can sometimes become very eager because of my theater/improv background and my management style. When I get excited, I can get ahead of myself and have a whole conversation that is over the head of my client. Living in the world of sales makes it easy to forget that not everyone understands the intricacies of my job. I used to feel the need to get my whole thought out before I could stop talking. I am now learning to listen. It is a work in progress and takes more concentration and focus to ACTUALLY listen than it does to open your mouth and talk. Listening allows one to successfully navigate the client relationship. When you get off of a call, you should be able to answer several questions about your client. What motivates them? Why are they *happy/unhappy with what I am providing them? What plan of action did I leave my client that I can later follow up on? Clients who believe you are listening to them will believe that you care about their business in the long-term relationship. Caring by listening keeps you at the front of the pack when the other suitors (vendors) come knocking at their door.*

Don't Let the Romance Die

Here's where things start to become challenging. You have a great relationship with your client where you talk to them every 90 days. You get complacent and think you know everything about them and how they run their business. Suddenly things change, and there's a new vendor in the picture. Maybe they still buy a couple of things from you, but someone else is coming along and taking another piece of their business. Over time, the new suitor could convert the whole account. The best way to overcome this challenge is to keep asking questions. What's new with you? I see that we have been taking care of X and Y for you, but we don't seem to have any Z on the books. Who takes care of that? Or sometimes, in lieu of candy and flowers, give your client a gratuitous discount or incentive. It's a small act of appreciation that will generate a great return for years to come. Letting the relationship die reflects poorly on the rep. We count on the recurring business to be our consistent base. When a client leaves, there is a reason for it. The reason is generally that the rep has let things slide, escalate, or someone else has swooped in and asked whether you have recently heard from your Toshiba rep. If that answer is longer than a quarter, then in the immortal words of Whoopi Goldberg, "Molly, you in danger, girl."

When Things Change – Let Them Know

This sounds like a no brainer, but one of the biggest fears that sales people have is communicating change to their clients. Prices increase over time, and most people understand that. Processes change both internally and externally. Change can be a hard pill to swallow, but being upfront and honest puts you in the best position to succeed. When things change you can feel confident asking questions and getting the honest answers in return.

Never Go Home Angry

The old adage is to "never go to bed angry". In my current working environment, I haven't seen anyone fall asleep. Handle your escalations by 5pm or whatever the end of your workday is. I prefer to handle them the moment they land on my desk or in my email. An angry person will stew in their juices if they are made to wait. They will create escape plans if you cannot provide a solution. I cannot tell you how many times I have called an angry client and closed the call with laughter and new business. Believe it or not, most escalations can be handled in one call. Sometimes it does take two calls or getting an expert involved. Letting those calls go for even one day can lengthen the resolution process. When clients are forced to wait, they begin to question whether it is worth the trouble in the first place. They may forgive the first time. They will pull away and eventually stop answering your calls if it becomes a trend.

Make Sure Any Split is Amicable so a Chance for Reconciliation Exists

Sondheim said it best when he said, "Sometimes people leave you (halfway through the wood)." Relationships with clients can eventually end. Sometimes there are irreconcilable differences or someone else, but sometimes it is YOU.

In the world of inside sales, it is your job to maintain these relationships. Your CRM and LinkedIn resources become your notes to maintain and build the relationship. Whether you are new or are passing the seven-year itch, you need to use your creative mind to keep things interesting. Even if the client moves on to another vendor, you can keep track of them and call out of the blue to ask how they are doing. Keep detailed notes to set up calls for major life events — marriages, having babies, graduations, and promotions. Those calls will remind them of why they wanted to work with you in the first place. This method makes the hard calls easier and the sales calls more fun. Your clients could find their way back to you if they believe you have their best interest at heart.

Spend time getting to know your clients. Understand what they do, what their challenges are, and offer solutions for what you can. Make sure these long-term relationships are secure and the lines of communication are open. One of our main focuses this year is to stay ahead of the curve by developing our predictive buying calendar for all of our regularly buying clients. The other part of that is keeping them happy so we can expand our business to include as many of the products and services we are able to offer across our entire company. We work as a team to ensure that a client gets the best in service when they choose to work with Toshiba.

CHAPTER 7

Communicating with Your Clients

A NYONE IN BUSINESS knows that the most important relation-ship is the one you have with the client. The client keeps the lights on, employees fed, and are the life blood of any business. No matter what you sell or whom you are selling to, the end game is always to get someone to buy-in and spend the dough on your idea, product, or service. Savvy sales peo-ple sell on value and build a loyal base of clients who be-come the foundation for growing the business. Non-savvy sales people drop the price and pester the clients to please just buy something now. Sometimes they will get a little deal, but they often won't. Sales people often forget that clients are sav-vy themselves. The potential client rarely thinks about how the product/service that is the sales reps' focus all day every day at work. Our job as sales people is to build a relationship and learn enough about our potential client's business to be able to communicate to them what our value would mean to their bottom line. That, my friends, is how you win business. That is also how you keep and expand business, compile refer-rals for new business, and generate testimonials for all of the wonderful business you have done. Easy, right? It sounds a lot easier than it is.

There are a lot of detailed and interactive sales trainings happening around the world today. Sales people are learning the steps of the sale, how to handle objections, and all types of creative closing techniques. Sales people are taught how to build rapport, when to quote new business, and every sneaky way possible to get a yes. I am working on a consultative approach with my team. We are sneaky in our own way. My team uses LinkedIn to learn about the people we are speaking with and connect with them to highlight both our professionalism and any common interests. It is nice to connect with someone who follows the same influencers you follow or belongs to some of the same groups. It is even better if you attended the same school. "You went to Furman University? So did I, please buy my product." It's not quite that simple, but having the ability to do research from one business media platform has proven to be efficient. LinkedIn is also a good place to follow their company and stay up to date on any press releases or major changes. Remember, people like to talk about themselves (and their companies). A warm conversation paves an easier path to the open-ended questions.

When it comes to communicating, the open-ended question is the key to opening many locked doors. Yes or no questions keep the sales rep talking. The more a sales rep talks on a call, the further they get from closing the deal. Having a general introduction, a purpose for the call, and a little structured small talk to build rapport is a necessary introduction. After that, you can approach open-ended questions. The next major key is to LISTEN. Too many humans spend their time preparing crafted responses during the critical time of listening. I am all about the prep work that goes into any situation, but you have to listen when a person is talking. They will provide all of the necessary clues to solve every mystery in life. How do I manage this person? Ask and listen. How do I get a first date? Ask and listen. How do I close a deal? Ask and listen. Have I mentioned that listening is a key part of effectively communicating with people? Be prepared, and listen once you enter into the conversation.

The next step is to pick up on cues to steer the conversation. Some people get so excited that they open the floodgates and data dump when they get into an actual conversation with a prospect. You have not won the deal yet. Ask thoughtful questions. Pick up on cues and steer the conversation. I need to be clear here – steer the existing conversation. Do not ask questions out of left field to highlight your own agenda. Let the conversation naturally lead you to the information you seek. When you get there, it will be from a willing participant who is building a relationship with you and not a hostage that you are interrogating. That willingness is important. Asking about a client's wedding, general health, or work life are ways to maintain a stronger connection.

Once trust has been built, you can let the client know it is time to order your product. Strategies include saying there is something new that made you think of them or that you are headed into a new role at a new company and want to take them with you. I am not saying that stealing business is okay, but my book of business relationships is my own, non-competes withstanding. When loyalty is built, it tends to remain. Competitors are calling your clients every day. If the relationship hangs on a financial string, it can easily break or be cut by a better sales professional.

The exercise for communicating with clients and prospects should be mandatory. You have to prepare more than ever until you have reached perfection. You then have to listen and skillfully direct the conversation. The last thing you have to do is ask for the business. Why go through the first several steps if you are not going to get what you came for?

A method I have found to be beneficial is the art of role-play. Employees are typically more invested in a role-play than the actual client is. My reps either go very hard on their partner or very easy. So the truest test is when they engage with the prospective buyer. Establishing a dialogue as they try to sell is crucial, but it requires active communication from both participants. Sales professionals reading this may even learn a thing or two.

People try to sell me things all of the time. I work for a big company. Other companies try selling sales software, marketing programs, or even attempt to recruit for me. You would think I'd have mercy on sales people, but I do not. I would not want them to have mercy on me. Growth comes from meeting challenges and exceeding expectations. I am never mean or impatient, but to earn my time you have to keep me engaged. If an applicant and I reach a place where we have active communication, I like the individual, and I am educated on his or her business, I will most likely hire that person.

After countless people attempted to sell me on related technology, I spoke with a young woman who started off with good conversation. She is now a friend and my go-to professional on all things that relate to her industry. Her sale began with a conversation and varied communication (over the phone, in person, and in emails). It ended in a handshake and a couple of prime-time engagements with my company.

Many of my sales heroes may slap me down for saying this, but this book is about what I believe. Prospects and clients will always have the upper hand.

If you want to win more business, learn how to talk to people. If that isn't the first skill in your bag of tricks, the rest of them will have little impact. We do not have to take subservient roles in these relationships. Part of the art of communication is realizing our role in any pairing. Are we the teacher, leader, mentor, friend, or the sales professional? You will see in each chapter that you are always the one asking the questions.

We spend our lives with answers on the tips of our tongues, ready to explain ourselves at the drop of a hat. What we really need to be doing is arming ourselves with thoughtful, evocative, and challenging questions. Those questions are meant for everyone we come into contact with, including ourselves. I meet interesting people every day. People define me as being a great friend, a wonderful colleague, and occasionally the life of the party. These descriptors are not meant as a backdoor brag, but as an illustration. I am known for these things because I invest in people with the revenue of questions. Once I know about people, can ask more insightful questions, and commit those answers to memory, people are drawn to me.

Remember when I said that I am only open enough to give out the little information I want to share in my own terms? Most people do not operate that way. They will show you every piece of dirty laundry they have because you showed enough interest to seemingly care. There is power in communicating on your own terms.

Teamwork Makes the Dream Work

❖

I would write less often if I did not have a group of coworkers who inspire me on a daily basis. I am blessed with a boss who mentors and challenges me. The senior leadership inspires my confidence by consistently supporting me, even when my ideas seem big or off-the-wall. Most of all, I am inspired by the team of people that I have the pleasure of managing. I have been truly inspired by their ideas and efforts as we laid out our business plan for 2015.

This is going to be a banner year! All of the work from the last couple of years has come to fruition in the form of new technology, ideas, and strategies for achieving new heights of success. Since we are a sales organization, I wanted to share some of the best ideas I have heard lately.

Become a Pro at Needs Analysis
The deepest penetration in our market requires the deepest level of knowledge about our customers. This knowledge allows us to build deep loyalty with those customers. Needs-analysis requires being prepared with the right questions that uncover information needed to best service our customers. The ultimate goal, more so than revenue closed, is the ongoing relationship. The end result is a customer that loyally buys from us and rejects our competition.

Take a Consultative Approach
"Checking in" or "touching base" with customers is my pet peeve. It is easy to constantly call and check in instead of actually getting to know

your customer's business. Taking a consultative approach to sales goes hand in hand with needs-analysis. The connotation of the word "consultant" implies that you are there to gather information and deliver expert advice for the customer. This is crucial in a sales role because taking a consultative approach to sales keeps you from leaving any opportunities on the table. Additionally, this approach is a great way to train customers how to buy. You can often just let them know that it is time to buy through succinct knowledge of their business and ordering history.

Leading Innovation

This is the motto of the company I work for; it is also my mantra. If we do not have something, we find it. If it does not exist, we build it. This year alone, the Aftermarket team led innovation in developing our CRM and developing it into an automated ordering system. Our team's goal of innovation is to expedite every process so we are able to focus on selling. In the past, the team was mired in administrative work. As we continue to innovate, the work gets faster. Working through one central CRM, we are able to get everything we need on one page. Having one point of access for the team keeps their workday moving and gives the management a plethora of data to organize and analyze.

Put Your Team Out Front

One of the best parts of having an innovative reputation is getting to take the lead on new projects. We have an exciting new marketing campaign coming up through a new partnership. We are the first to develop, automate, and use our CRM. We are jumping into the world of social selling. The whole team spends time reading and researching sales methodology. When a great idea is presented, we are allowed to run with it.

Professional Development

A team that reads, studies, and is constantly looking for avenues of professional development is a winning team. When reps look for opportunities to get more educated on products and processes, they add to the overall success of the team. Professional development is not something that searches you out. One must go out and get the opportunity. One of my best new team members approached me about getting more information on a product that we have amazing access to and that generates a lot of gross profit. Many sales reps tend to avoid complicated sales. In this reps case, he strived to be an expert and was rewarded by landing the client. His approach is now a key part of his development plan.

Social Selling

I have been social selling for over five years now. I have thousands of connections on LinkedIn that I have worked both with and for. The faces of my connections represent a lot of the business I have earned through the years. Now that social selling is on the road map for my team's 2015 plan, we are bringing in a consultant to ensure that everyone is prepared, understands social selling, and is able to use it as a business closing tool. For this year, I have implemented a bonus for the rep that is able to generate the most revenue through social selling.

Understand the Impact of Gross Profit

Revenue is great. Big numbers are ones that impress, but gross profit is what we walk away with. This year we have a focus on gross profit and pricing strategies. Gouging customers is unethical and giving away the farm shows lack of skill. The goal is to find the magic number where we are both profitable and competitive. Using our big bag of tools, we look to be a consultative salesperson who uses analytics to win over ALL of a customer's business. The more business you are able to earn from a recurring customer, the more places you can find to balance their savings with your gross profit.

Make Everyone a Part of the TEAM

The team mentality is a game changer. It started out with our small Aftermarket crew, but now we are spreading the team mentality across the entire organization. The Aftermarket reps help equipment reps and technicians. It is an "all for one and one for all" approach to have the best customer service. The more people who buy in to the team mentality, the stronger your team becomes.

We have suddenly become stacked with experts, closers, vendors, and admins who want to work with us. People all over the organization are now willing to share best-practices and take on challenging situations in the name of being team players.

Accept, Adjust, and Adapt to Change

Change is a constant. Business flounders and things grow stale when leaders are reluctant to change processes. I prefer salespeople to "stales-people" any day. When something new comes around the bend for us, we know we can leverage it to close more business and grow our market share. The team accepts that change is constant, and they must adjust and adapt to whatever the new system is.

Close with Kindness

At the end of the day, we are a sales organization. Our company's success boils down to the business we are able to close. A culture of happiness is fostered when a happy team enjoys each other, shares their wealth of knowledge, and feels comfortable enough to depend on one another. Kindness is inspired when you are happy about the people you work with. A culture of appreciation and kindness inevitably flows into the relationships with customers. What could be better than closing a deal with kindness? Nothing inspires more loyalty than when a customer feels both taken care of and appreciated.

I am always bragging about my team because they are the real deal. I am lucky to have them. Their results speak for themselves. The old school thinking of team members competing against one another to drive numbers is not something I buy into anymore. I can make a case by the numbers and the company culture, that teamwork makes the dream work.

How NOT To Be Terrible At Sales

❖

The profession of sales often gets a bad rap. Most people hear the word and associate it with a used car dealer or the person who follows them around the store using "tactics" to force an impulsive buying choice for the consumer.

I get a great deal of fulfillment from combining an arsenal of personal skills and learned tools to drive sales. I believe that sales is a noble profession. I do, however, think that there are many people in the field who do not understand how to get the most out of it. What follows is a guide detailing how to NOT be terrible at sales.

First let me set the stage. This sales job has a base salary. You get paid for showing up. There is a benefits package with paid time off and insurance. A lot of employment perks end right there; people work 40 hours a week and enjoy the ceiling of their salary and benefits. Sales has the added benefit of commission, bonuses, incentives, and all kinds of accelerators for overachievement.

Sales is a field where you can earn as much as you are willing to work for. Why do some sales people not want to do the work? If I knew that 50 calls would get me to a comfortable living, but 100 calls would get me to a six-figure income, why wouldn't I make 100 calls every day?

Stop Making Excuses

The number one reason that sales people are not more successful is that they make excuses. We are all in control of our choices. Even the most micromanaged worker in an office has control over their output of work. I have spent too many hours listening to excuses in my years as a manager. People bring their personal issues to work, blame the processes that are in place, and blame the company that hired and trained them.

In order to be successful, you must know what you need to get done. If you do not have the skills or tools to be successful, management is required to find a more suitable position for you or act as a coach until the skills are learned.

Sales is about THE WORK

There are jobs out there where you can give minimal effort from time to time. Sales is not one of those jobs. Sales requires attention every day. Prospects and clients must be called, product knowledge must be consistent, metrics must be met, and quotas must be hit. The calls you didn't make today are deals you aren't going to close tomorrow. Like any other field, there is a tipping point in the profession of sales. When relationships are strong and numbers are consistent, you can feel confident about being where you need to be. It takes years of hard work and deep relationships to get to that point. There are always competitors outworking you and calling clients to ask how long it's been since they've heard from you. If your manager gives you a workable plan and shows you how to be successful, do the work. If they are good at their job and knowledgeable about the industry, you will likely get to where you need to be.

Commit to the Process

There will always be new ideas about how to sell. Social selling is new and exciting, some people really do prefer only to be contacted via email.

Sales leaders hear it all. I didn't have to make any calls today because people were calling and emailing me. I didn't close any business today, but I made so many great new connections. I know I'm behind my pace, but I am about to pull in a whale that is going to make my number for the year. All of these things are great, but that does not change the expectation or the process.

The first step in your process should be to have a plan. That plan includes calls, quotes, daily pace, and any other expected metric. You then work the plan and call your prospects and clients. You use your tools and skills to provide quotes, close the business, and look for opportunities to expand. Outside of those parameters, doing anything else during the course of the day is a waste of time. Mediocre salespeople are always using self-created administrative work as an excuse for not being more successful.

Go ALL IN

Anything worth doing in life is worth doing well.

When your living is at stake, you should be putting in 100% effort every day. Since sales jobs have quotas and not meeting those quotas can result in losing your livelihood, every day should be ALL IN. Help should be on the way if you work the plan and still fall short. If you give a half-hearted effort, you shouldn't expect to keep your seat. If you love your job and work for a great company and go ALL IN, you should be able to make a fantastic living.

My company has great products, amazing relationships with dedicated vendors, engaged leadership, innovative ideas, and an HR policy that makes sure every employees have multiple chances to succeed.

If you are on my team, the only thing stopping you from success is the work that you are willing to put in.

Sales requires a rare balance of creativity and analytics. One must fully engage both sides of the brain. It revolves around relationships yet has multiple avenues for professional development. If you identify yourself as a sales professional, be a professional and DO THE WORK. Doing the work is the only thing that will get you paid.

Conclusion

W E WENT THROUGH all of the different ways that I have found success through communication. Communication allows you to know yourself and be a concerned friend and relative. It helps you set yourself apart in your career and build strong internal relationships to establish yourself as a creative and innovative thinker. It helps you build strong and fruitful relationships with vendor partners and clients. Preparation, listening, and building up the confidence to ask for what you want or need are all aspects of being a good communicator. You will get into great communicative shape if you put these exercises into practice and commit to them.

When my team is reaching out to anyone, I tell them to offer whatever they can before asking for anything in return. Simply say, "If there is anything I can ever do for you, please don't hesitate to let me know." Being genuine is integral. When people ask for favors, do your best to do them. Do not over extend yourself into a life of servitude, but donate your time when you can.

My team is successful because they communicate. They also prepare, do favors, and share information with each other. They use their creative minds, listen, and ask for business. That is all it really takes.

www.ingramcontent.com/pod-product-compliance
Lightning Source LLC
Chambersburg PA
CBHW031949190326
41519CB00007B/730